Tudor and Stuart Love Songs

Edited by J. Potter Briscoe

TUDOR AND STUART LOVE SONGS

SELECTED AND EDITED BY

J. POTTER BRISCOE, F.R.S.L.

Editor of "The Bibelots"

INTRODUCTION.

The spirit of reform which was developed during the early part of the sixteenth century brought about a desire on the part of young men of means to travel on the continent of Europe. This was for the purpose of making themselves acquainted with the politics, social life, literature, art, science, and commerce of the various nations of the same, especially of France, Spain, and Italy. These young Englishmen on their return introduced into the society in which they mixed not only the politenesses of these countries, but the wit of Italy, and the character of the poetry which was then in vogue in Southern Europe. Among these travellers during the reign of Henry the Eighth were Sir Thomas Wyatt and the Earl of Surrey. These courtiers possessed the poetical faculty, and therefore paid special attention to literary form. As a result they introduced the Sonnet of the Petrarchan type into England. The amorous verse of the inhabitants of these sunny climes took hold of the young Englishmen. Many men of rank and education, who did not regard themselves as of the world of letters, penned pleasant verse, much of it being of an amatory character based upon that of the Italians. During the reign of "Good Queen Bess" England was full of song. Of the writers of love verses William Watson occupied a very high, probably the highest, position during the time of Elizabeth. A glance at the Table of Contents of this volume will show that some of the best poets who were born between the years 1503 and 1679 have handed down to us poetical contributions of this character.

Of the Elizabethan amatory verses only a small portion has been transmitted to us. That which possessed least literary merit did not long survive, and, no doubt, some of considerable merit has been lost too. The best has been preserved. Selections from these, arranged in chronological order, appear in this anthology. Richard Tottel printed his "Miscellany" in 1557. It is to this work, and to Richard Edwards' "Paradise of Dainty Devices, " issued nineteen years later, that much of the best poetical literature of the sixteenth century has come down to us. The first-named passed through eight editions during thirty years: the last issue being dated 1587.

From the amatory verses produced by seventy-one writers during the reign of Henry the Eighth and down to those of the early Georges one hundred and thirteen appear in this love anthology. The limitation of space prevents further biographical particulars being given than the years of birth and death, which will be found in the Table of Contents. As writers do not always agree in this respect, "The Dictionary of National Biography" has been taken as the authority.

Whatever labour has been bestowed on the preparation of this anthology has not been in bulking it out to its present dimensions, but rather in keeping it within the prescribed limits; and, at the same time, furnishing these best examples of the love verses of the numerous authors who have been requisitioned for the purpose of this volume of "Tudor and Stuart Love Songs. "

J. P. B.

CONTENTS.

Robert Southwell (1561?-1595).
  Love's servile lot

Sir John Harrington (1561-1612).
  The heart of stone

Henry Constable (1561-1613).
  A shepherd's song to his love

Samuel Daniel (1562-1619).
  Love now, for roses fade
  Early love
  Love is a sickness

Christopher Marlowe (1564-1593).
  The passionate shepherd to his love

Joshua Sylvester (1563-1618).
  Love's omnipresence

Michael Drayton (1563-1631).
  A parting, or Love's last chance

William Shakespeare (1564-1616).
  Who is Silvia?
  Sigh no more, ladies
  A morning song for Imogen

Anon. (*circa* 1564).
  The unfaithful shepherdess

Anon.
  True loveliness
  A woman's reason

Love will find out the way
Phillida flouts me
In praise of two

Sir Robert Aytoun (1570-1638).
  To his forsaken mistress
  On women's inconstancy

Thomas Middleton (1570?-1627).
  The three states of women
  My love and I must part

Ben Jonson (1573?-1637).
  Perfect beauty
  To Celia

Dr. John Donne (1573-1631).
  A woman's constancy
  Sweetest love

William Alexander, Earl of Stirling (1567?-1640).
  To Aurora

William Drummond (1585-1649).
  Phillis

Beaumont and Fletcher (1584-1616; 1579-1625).
  Take those lips away

Francis Beaumont (1584-1616).
  Tell me what is love
  Pining for love
  Fie on love

John Wootton (*circa* 1600).
  Damoetas' praise of his Daphnis

George Wither (1588-1667).
  Shall I, wasting in despair

Thomas Carew (1598?-1639?).
  To one who, when I praised my mistress'
    beauty, said I was blind
  He that loves a rosy cheek

Nathaniel Field (1587-   ).
  Matin song

Robert Herrick (1591-1674).
  Julia
  Cherry ripe
  To the virgins
  To Electra

Bp. Henry King (1592-1669).
  Dry those eyes

John Dowland (ed.) (1563?-1626?).
  True till death

Thomas Weelkes (ed.) (1597-   ?).
  Farewell, my joy

Sir William Davenant (1605-1606-1668).
  The lark now leaves

Edmund Waller (1606-1687).
  Go, lovely rose!

Thomas Randolph (1605-1635).
  His mistress

Henry Vaughan (1622-1695).
  Chloris

Anon. (*circa* 1610).
  Love me little, love me long

Capt. Tobias Hume (musical composer).
  Fain would I change that note

William Habington.
  To roses in Castara's breast

John Danyel (1604?-1625?).
  Thou pretty bird

Anon. (*temp.* James I.).
  Once I lov'd a maiden fair

Sir John Suckling (1609-1642).
  I pr'ythee send me back my heart
  Orsame's song—"Why so pale," etc.

Thomas Ford, composer (1607?-1648).
  Since first I saw your face

Abraham Cowley (1618-1667).
  The given heart

Sir Edward Sherburne (1618-1702).
  Ice and fire

Richard Lovelace (1618-1658).
  Amarantha
  To Althea, from prison

Alexander Brome (1620-1666).
  A mock song

Thomas Stanley (1625-1678).
  Speaking and kissing

Sir George Etherege (1635?-1691).
  Ladies' conquering eyes

Charles Sackville, Earl of Dorset (1638-1706).
  Dorinda

Robert Gould (-1709?).
  Celia and Sylvia

Sir Charles Sedley (1639?-1701).
  True love

John Wilmot, Earl of Rochester (1647-1680).
  Too late!
  My mistress' heart
  Constancy

Peter Anthony Motteux (1660-1718).
  Man and woman

Matthew Prior (1664-1721).
  Accept my heart

Sir John Vanbrugh (1664-1726).
  An angelic woman
  I smile at love

George Granville (1667-1735).
  Adieu l'amour

William Congreve (1670-1729).
  Sabina wakes
  Inconstancy

Ambrose Philips (1675?-1709).
  Love and hate

John Oldmixon (1673-1742).
  I lately vowed

Dr. Isaac Watts (1674-1748).
  Few happy matches

John Hughes (1677-1720).
  Dorinda's conquest

George Farquhar (1678-1707).
  Lovers in disguise

Thomas Parnell (1679-1718).
  When thy beauty appears

THE LOST HEART.

Help me to seek! For I lost it there;
And, if that ye have found it, ye that be here,
And seek to convey it secretly,
Handle it soft and treat it tenderly,
Or else it will 'plain, and then appair.
  But pray restore it mannerly,
Since that I do ask it thus honestly;
For to lose it, it sitteth me near;
  Help me to seek!

Alas, and is there no remedy?
But have I thus lost it wilfully?
I-wis, it was a thing all too dear
To be bestowed, and wist not where!
It was mine heart! I pray you heartily
  Help me to seek!

Sir Thomas Wyatt.

THE LOVER'S APPEAL.

And wilt thou leave me thus?
Say nay! say nay! for shame,
To save thee from the blame
Of all my grief and grame.
And wilt thou leave me thus?
Say nay! say nay!

And wilt thou leave me thus,
That hath loved thee so long
In wealth and woe among:
And is thy heart so strong
As for to leave me thus?
Say nay! say nay!

And wilt thou leave me thus,
That hath given thee my heart

Never for to depart
Neither for pain nor smart:
And wilt thou leave me thus?
Say nay! say nay!

And wilt thou leave me thus,
And have no more pity
Of him that loveth thee?
Alas! thy cruelty!
And wilt thou leave me thus?
Say nay! say nay!

Sir Thomas Wyatt.

A SONNET.

Love, that liveth and reigneth in my thought,
That built his seat within my captive breast,
Clad in the arms wherein with me he fought,
Oft in my face he doth his banner rest:
She that me taught to love and suffer pain,
My doubtful hope and eke my hot desire
With shamefaced cloak to shadow and restrain,
Her smiling grace converteth straight to ire:
And coward Love then to the heart apace
Taketh his flight, whereas he lurks and plains
His purpose lost, and dare not show his face.
For my lord's guilt, thus faultless, bide I pains:
    Yet from my lord shall not my foot remove;
    Sweet is his death that takes his end by love!

Henry Howard, Earl of Surrey.

A VOW TO LOVE FAITHFULLY HOWSOEVER HE BE REWARDED.

Set me whereas the sun doth parch the green,
Or where his beams do not dissolve the ice,
In temperate heat where he is felt and seen,
In presence pressed of people mad or wise,
Set me in high, or yet in low degree,
In longest night, or in the shortest day,
In clearest sky, or where clouds thickest be,
In lusty youth, or when my hairs are gray,
Set me in heaven, in earth, or else in hell,
In hill or dale, or in the foaming flood,
Thrall, or at large, alive whereso I dwell,
Sick, or in health, in evil fame or good:
Hers will I be, and only with this thought
Content myself, although my chance be nought.

Henry Howard, Earl of Surrey.

3

MY SWEET SWEETING.

Ah, my sweet sweeting!
  My little pretty sweeting,
My sweeting will I love wherever I go:
  She is so proper and pure,
Full steadfast, stable, and demure,
  There is none such, you may be sure,
    As my sweet sweeting.

In all this world, as thinketh me,
Is none so pleasant to my eye,
That I am glad so oft to see
    As my sweet sweeting.

When I behold my sweeting sweet,
Her face, her hands, her mignon feet,
They seem to me there is none so sweet
    As my sweet sweeting.

Anon., circa 1530.

THE LOVER TO HIS LADY.

My girl, thou gazest much
   Upon the golden skies:
Would *I* were Heaven! I would behold
   Thee then with all mine eyes!

George Turberville.

MASTER GEORGE: HIS SONNET OF THE PAINS OF LOVE.

Two lines shall tell the grief
   That I by love sustain:
I burn, I flame, I faint, I freeze,
   Of Hell I feel the pain.

George Turberville.

TURBERVILLE'S ANSWER AND DISTICH TO THE SAME.

Two lines shall teach you how
   To purchase love anew:
Let reason rule, where Love did reign,
   And idle thoughts eschew.

George Turberville.

THE SHEPHERD'S COMMENDATION OF HIS NYMPH.

What shepherd can express
The favour of her face
To whom, in this distress,
I do appeal for grace?
  A thousand Cupids fly
  About her gentle eye;

From which each throws a dart,
That kindleth soft sweet fire
Within my sighing heart,
Possessed by desire:
  No sweeter life I try
  Than in her love to die!

The lily in the field,
That glories in his white,
For pureness now must yield
And render up his right;
  Heaven pictured in her face
  Doth promise joy and grace.

Fair Cynthia's silver light,
That beats on running streams,
Compares not with her white,
Whose hairs are all sunbeams:
  So bright my Nymph doth shine
  As day unto my eyne!

With this, there is a red,
Exceeds the damask-rose,
Which in her cheeks is spread,
Where every favour grows;
  In sky there is no star,
  But she surmounts it far.

When Phoebus from the bed
Of Thetis doth arise,
The morning, blushing red,
In fair carnation-wise,

He shows in my Nymph's face,
As Queen of every grace.

This pleasant lily-white,
This taint of roseate red,
This Cynthia's silver light,
This sweet fair Dea spread,
  These sunbeams in mine eye,
  These beauties, make me die!

Edward Vere, Earl of Oxford.

A RENUNCIATION.

If women could be fair, and yet not fond,
Or that their love were firm, not fickle still,
I would not marvel that they make men bond
By service long to purchase their good will;
But when I see how frail those creatures are,
I muse that men forget themselves so far.

To mark the choice they make, and how they change,
How oft from Phoebus they do flee to Pan;
Unsettled still, like haggards wild they range,
These gentle birds that fly from man to man;
Who would not scorn and shake them from the fist,
And let them fly, fair fools, which way they list?

Yet for disport we fawn and flatter both,
To pass the time when nothing else can please,
And train them to our lure with subtle oath,
Till, weary of their wiles, ourselves we ease;
And then we say when we their fancy try,
To play with fools, O what a fool was I!

Edward Vere, Earl of Oxford.

THE COMPLAINT OF HARPALUS.

Phylida was a fair maid
And fresh as any flower,
Whom Harpalus the herdman prayed
To be his paramour.
 Harpalus and eke Corin
Were herdmen, both yfere;
And Phylida could twist and spin,
And thereto sing full clear.
 But Phylida was all too coy
For Harpalus to win;
For Corin was her only joy,
Who forced her not a pin.
 How often would she flowers twine,
How often garlands make,
Of cowslips and of columbine,
And all for Corin's sake!
 But Corin, he had hawks to lure,
And forced more the field;
Of lovers' law he took no cure,
For once he was beguiled.
 Harpalus prevailed nought;
His labour all was lost;
For he was farthest from her thoughts,
And yet he loved her most.
 Therefore waxed he both pale and lean,
And dry as clot of clay;
His flesh it was consumed clean,
His colour gone away....
 His beasts he kept upon the hill,
And he sate in the dale;
And thus, with sighs and sorrows shrill,
He gan to tell his tale.
 "O Harpalus," — thus would he say —
"Unhappiest under sun,
The cause of thine unhappy day
By love was first begun!...
 O Cupid, grant this my request,
And do not stop thine ears,
That she may feel within her breast

The pains of my despairs!
   Of Corin that is careless,
That she may crave her fee,
As I have done in great distress,
That loved her faithfully!" ...

Barnaby Googe (?).

A STRANGE PASSION OF A LOVER.

Amid my bale I bathe in bliss,
I swim in Heaven, I sink in hell:
I find amends for every miss,
And yet my moan no tongue can tell.
I live and love (what would you more?)
As never lover lived before.

I laugh sometimes with little lust,
So jest I oft and feel no joy;
Mine eye is builded all on trust,
And yet mistrust breeds mine annoy.
I live and lack, I lack and have;
I have and miss the thing I crave.

  * * * * *

Then like the lark that passed the night
In heavy sleep with cares oppressed;
Yet when she spies the pleasant light,
She sends sweet notes from out her breast;
So sing I now because I think
How joys approach when sorrows shrink.

And as fair Philomene again
Can watch and sing when others sleep;
And taketh pleasure in her pain,
To wray the woe that makes her weep;
So sing I now for to bewray
The loathsome life I lead alway.

The which to thee, dear wench, I write,
Thou know'st my mirth but not my moan;
I pray God grant thee deep delight,
To live in joys when I am gone.
I cannot live; it will not be:
I die to think to part from thee.

George Gascoigne.

10

TO PHYLLIS, THE FAIR SHEPHERDESS.

My Phyllis hath the morning sun
  At first to look upon her:
And Phyllis hath morn-waking birds
  Her rising still to honour.
My Phyllis hath prime feathered flowers
  That smile when she treads on them:
And Phyllis hath a gallant flock
  That leaps since she doth own them.
But Phyllis hath too hard a heart,
  Alas, that she should have it!
It yields no mercy to desert
  Nor peace to those that crave it.
Sweet Sun, when thou look'st on,
  Pray her regard my moan!
Sweet birds, when you sing to her,
  To yield some pity woo her!
Sweet flowers, that she treads on,
  Tell her, her beauty dreads one;
And if in life her love she'll not agree me,
  Pray her before I die, she will come see me.

Sir Edward Dyer.

THE ENAMOURED SHEPHERD.

O gentle Love, ungentle for thy deed!
    Thou mak'st my heart
    A bloody mark,
With piercing shot to bleed.

Shoot soft, sweet Love! for fear thou shoot amiss,
    For fear too keen
    Thy arrows been,
And hit the heart where my Beloved is.

Too fair that fortune were, nor never I
    Shall be so blest,
    Among the rest,
That Love shall seize on her by sympathy.

Then since with Love my prayers bear no boot,
    This doth remain
    To cease my pain:
I take the wound, and die at Venus' foot.

George Peele.

HIS LOVE ADMITS NO RIVAL.

Shall I like a hermit dwell,
On a rock, or in a cell,
Calling home the smallest part
That is missing of my heart,
To bestow it where I may
Meet a rival every day?
If she undervalue me,
What care I how fair she be?

Were her tresses angel gold,
If a stranger may be bold,
Unrebuked, unafraid,
To convert them to a braid,
And with little more ado
Work them into bracelets too?
If the mine be grown so free,
What care I how rich it be?

Were her hand as rich a prize
As her hairs, or precious eyes,
If she lay them out to take
Kisses, for good manners' sake:
And let every lover skip
From her hand unto her lip;
If she seem not chaste to me,
What care I how chaste she be?

No; she must be perfect snow,
In effect as well as show;
Warming, but as snowballs do,
Not like fire, by burning too;
But when she by change hath got
To her heart a second lot,
Then if others share with me,
Farewell her, whate'er she be!

Sir Walter Raleigh.

THE SHEPHERD'S DESCRIPTION OF LOVE.

"Shepherd, what's love? I pray thee tell!" —
It is that fountain, and that well,
Where pleasure and repentance dwell;
It is, perhaps, that passing bell
That tolls us all to heaven or hell;
And this is love, as I heard tell.

"Yet, what is love? good shepherd, saine!" —
It is a sunshine mix'd with rain;
It is a toothache, or like pain;
It is a game where none doth gain:
The lass saith No, and would full fain!
And this is love, as I hear saine.

"Yet, shepherd, what is love, I pray?" —
It is a "Yea," it is a "Nay,"
A pretty kind of sporting fray;
It is a thing will soon away;
Then, nymphs, take vantage while ye may,
And this is love, as I hear say.

"Yet what is love? good shepherd, show!" —
A thing that creeps, it cannot go,
A prize that passeth to and fro,
A thing for one, a thing for moe;
And he that proves shall find it so;
And, shepherd, this is love, I trow.

Sir Walter Raleigh.

THE SHEPHERDESS'S REPLY TO THE PASSIONATE SHEPHERD.

If all the world and Love were young,
And truth in every shepherd's tongue,
These pretty pleasures might me move
To live with thee and be thy love.

But time drives flocks from field to fold,
When rivers rage, and rocks grow cold;
Then Philomel becometh dumb,
The rest complains of cares to come.

The flowers do fade, and wanton fields
To wayward winter reckoning yields;
A honey tongue, a heart of gall,
Is fancy's spring: but sorrow's fall.

Thy gowns, thy shoes, thy bed of roses,
Thy cup, thy kirtle, and thy posies,
Soon break, soon wither, soon forgotten; —
In folly ripe, in reason rotten.

The belt of straw and ivy-buds,
Thy coral clasps and amber studs, —
All these in me no means can move,
To come to thee, and be thy love.

What should we talk of dainties, then,
Of better meat than's fit for men?
These are but vain: that's only good
Which God hath bless'd and sent for food.

But could youth last, and love still breed;
Had joys no date, nor age no need;
Then those delights my mind might move,
To live with thee, and be thy love.

Sir Walter Raleigh.

[See "The Passionate Shepherd to His Love]

LOVE FOR LOVE.

Away with these self-loving lads
Whom Cupid's arrow never glads!
Away, poor souls, that sigh and weep,
In love of them that lie and sleep!
  For Cupid is a merry god,
  And forceth none to kiss the rod.

Sweet Cupid's shafts, like Destiny,
Do causeless good or ill decree;
Desert is borne out of his bow,
Reward upon his wing doth go:
  What fools are they that have not known
  That Love likes no laws but his own!

My songs, they be of Cynthia's praise:
I wear her rings on holy days;
On every tree I write her name,
And every day I read the same:
  Where Honour Cupid's rival is,
  There miracles are seen of his.

If Cynthia crave her ring of me,
I blot her name out of the tree;
If doubt do darken things held dear,
Then "farewell nothing," once a year:
  For many run, but one must win;
  Fools only hedge the cuckoo in.

The worth that worthiness should move
Is love, which is the due of love;
And love as well the shepherd can
As can the mighty nobleman: —
  Sweet nymph, 'tis true, you worthy be;
  Yet, without love, nought worth to me.

Fulke-Greville, Lord Brooke.

CUPID AND MY CAMPASPE: APELLES' SONG.

Cupid and my Campaspe played
At cards for kisses: Cupid paid.
He stakes his quiver, bows and arrows,
His mother's doves and team of sparrows;
Loses them too; then down he throws
The coral of his lip, the rose
Growing on 's cheek, but none knows how;
With these the crystal of his brow,
And then the dimple of his chin—
All these did my Campaspe win.
At last he set her both his eyes.—
She won, and Cupid blind did rise.
O Love, has she done this to thee?
What shall, alas! become of me?

John Lyly.

A DITTY.

My true-love hath my heart, and I have his,
By just exchange one to the other given:
I hold his dear, and mine he cannot miss,
There never was a better bargain driven:
  My true-love hath my heart, and I have his.

His heart in me keeps him and me in one,
My heart in him his thoughts and senses guides:
He loves my heart, for once it was his own,
I cherish his because in me it bides:
  My true-love hath my heart, and I have his.

Sir Philip Sidney.

LOVE IS DEAD.

Ring out your bells, let mourning shews be spread;
For Love is dead:
    All Love is dead, infected
With plague of deep disdain:
    Worth, as nought worth, rejected,
And Faith fair scorn doth gain.
    From so ungrateful fancy,
    From such a female franzy,
    From them that use men thus,
    Good Lord, deliver us!

Weep, neighbours, weep; do you not hear it said
That Love is dead?
    His death-bed, peacock's folly;
His winding-sheet is shame;
    His will, false-seeming holy;
His sole executor, blame.
    From so ungrateful fancy,
    From such a female franzy,
    From them that use men thus,
    Good Lord, deliver us!

Let dirge be sung, and trentals rightly read,
For Love is dead;
    Sir Wrong his tomb ordaineth
My mistress' marble heart;
    Which epitaph containeth,
Her eyes were once his dart.
    From so ungrateful fancy,
    From such a female franzy,
    From them that use men thus,
    Good Lord, deliver us!

Alas, I lie; rage hath this error bred;
Love is not dead;
    Love is not dead, but sleepeth
In his unmatched mind,
    Where she his counsel keepeth,
Till due deserts she find:

Therefore from so vile fancy,
To call such wit a franzy,
Who Love can temper thus,
Good Lord, deliver us!

Sir Philip Sidney.

HE THAT LOVES.

He that loves and fears to try,
Learns his mistress to deny.
Doth she chide thee? 'tis to show it
That thy coldness makes her do it.
Is she silent, is she mute?
Silence fully grants thy suit.
Doth she pout and leave the room?
Then she goes to bid thee come.

Is she sick? why then be sure
She invites thee to the cure.
Doth she cross thy suit with "No"?
Tush! she loves to hear thee woo.
Doth she call the faith of men
In question? nay, she loves thee then,
And if e'er she makes a blot,
She's lost if that thou hit'st her not.

He that after ten denials
Doth attempt no further trials,
Hath no warrant to acquire
The dainties of his chaste desire.

Sir Philip Sidney.

LOVE'S WANTONNESS.

Love guards the roses of thy lips,
  And flies about them like a bee:
If I approach, he forward skips,
  And if I kiss, he stingeth me.
Love in thine eyes doth build his bower,
  And sleeps within their pretty shine;
And if I look, the boy will lower,
  And from their orbs shoot shafts divine.
Love works thy heart within his fire,
  And in my tears doth firm the same;
And if I tempt, it will retire,
  And of my plaints doth make a game.
Love, let me cull her choicest flowers,
  And pity me, and calm her eye;
Make soft her heart, dissolve her lowers,
  Then will I praise thy deity,
But if thou do not, Love, I'll truly serve her
In spite of thee, and by firm faith deserve her.

Thomas Lodge.

ROSALINE.

Like to the clear in highest sphere
Where all imperial glory shines,
Of selfsame colour is her hair
Whether unfolded, or in twines:
  Heigh ho, fair Rosaline!
Her eyes are sapphires set in snow,
Resembling heaven by every wink;
The Gods do fear whenas they glow,
And I do tremble when I think
  Heigh ho, would she were mine!

Her cheeks are like the blushing cloud
That beautifies Aurora's face,
Or like the silver crimson shroud

21

That Phoebus' smiling looks doth grace;
  Heigh ho, fair Rosaline!
Her lips are like two budded roses
Whom ranks of lilies neighbour nigh,
Within which bounds she balm encloses
Apt to entice a deity:
  Heigh ho, would she were mine!

Her neck is like a stately tower
Where Love himself imprison'd lies,
To watch for glances every hour
From her divine and sacred eyes:
  Heigh ho, for Rosaline!
Her paps are centres of delight,
Her breasts are orbs of heavenly frame,
Where Nature moulds the dew of light
To feed perfection with the same:
  Heigh ho, would she were mine!

With orient pearl, with ruby red,
With marble white, with sapphire blue
Her body every way is fed,
Yet soft in touch and sweet in view:
  Heigh ho, fair Rosaline!
Nature herself her shape admires;
The Gods are wounded in her sight;
And Love forsakes his heavenly fires
And at her eyes his brand doth light:
  Heigh ho, would she were mine!

Then muse not, Nymphs, though I bemoan
The absence of fair Rosaline,
Since for a fair there's fairer none,
Nor for her virtues so divine:
  Heigh ho, fair Rosaline;
Heigh ho, my heart! would God that she were mine!

Thomas Lodge.

THE MAY QUEEN.

With fragrant flowers we strew the way,
And make this our chief holiday;
For though this clime were blest of yore,
Yet was it never proud before.
  O beauteous Queen of second Troy,
  Accept of our unfeigned joy!

Now th' air is sweeter than sweet balm,
And satyrs dance about the palm;
Now earth, with verdure newly dight,
Gives perfect signs of her delight.
  O beauteous Queen of second Troy,
  Accept of our unfeigned joy!

Now birds recall new harmony,
And trees do whistle melody;
Now everything that nature breeds,
Doth clad itself in pleasant weeds.
  O beauteous Queen of second Troy,
  Accept of our unfeigned joy!

Thomas Watson.

PHILLIDA AND CORYDON.

In the merry month of May,
In a morn by break of day,
With a troop of damsels playing,
Forth I rode, forsooth, a-maying,
When anon by a woodside,
Where as May was in his pride,
I espied, all alone,
Phillida and Corydon.

Much ado there was, God wot!
He would love, and she would not:
She said, never man was true:
He said, none was false to you.
He said, he had loved her long:
She said, love should have no wrong.

Corydon would kiss her then,
She said, maids must kiss no men,
Till they do for good and all;
Then she made the shepherd call
All the heavens to witness truth,
Never loved a truer youth.

Thus with many a pretty oath,
Yea, and nay, and faith and troth,
Such as silly shepherds use
When they will not love abuse;
Love, which had been long deluded,
Was with kisses sweet concluded:
And Phillida with garlands gay,
Was made the lady of the May.

Richard Breton.

SHALL I COME, SWEET LOVE?

Shall I come, sweet Love, to thee
  When the evening beams are set?
Shall I not excluded be,
  Will you find no feigned let?
Let me not, for pity, more
Tell the long hours at your door.

Who can tell what thief or foe,
  In the covert of the night,
For his prey will work my woe,
  Or through wicked foul despite?
So may I die unredrest
Ere my long love be possest.

But to let such dangers pass,
  Which a lover's thoughts disdain,
'Tis enough in such a place
  To attend love's joys in vain:
Do not mock me in thy bed,
While these cold nights freeze me dead.

Thomas Campion.

CHERRY-RIPE.

There is a garden in her face
  Where roses and white lilies blow;
A heavenly paradise that place,
  Wherein all pleasant fruits do grow;
There cherries grow that none may buy,
Till Cherry-Ripe themselves do cry.

Those cherries fairly do enclose
  Of orient pearl a double row,
Which when her lovely laughter shows,
  They look like rose-buds fill'd with snow.
Yet them no peer nor prince may buy,

Till Cherry-Ripe themselves do cry.

Her eyes like angels watch them still;
  Her brows like bended bows do stand,
Threat'ning with piercing frowns to kill
  All that approach with eye or hand
These sacred cherries to come nigh,
Till Cherry-Ripe themselves do cry.

Thomas Campion.

FAIR SAMELA.

Like to Diana in her summer weed,
Girt with a crimson robe of brightest dye,
      Goes fair Samela;

Whiter than be the flocks that straggling feed,
When wash'd by Arethusa's fount they lie,
      Is fair Samela;

As fair Aurora in her morning gray,
Deck'd with the ruddy glister of her love,
      Is fair Samela;

Like lovely Thetis on a calmed day,
Whenas her brightness Neptune's fancy move,
      Shines fair Samela;

Her tresses gold, her eyes like glassy streams,
Her teeth are pearl, the breasts are ivory
      Of fair Samela;

Her cheeks, like rose and lily, yield forth gleams,
Her brows, bright arches fram'd of ebony;
      Thus fair Samela

Passeth fair Venus in her bravest hue,
And Juno in the show of majesty,
      (For she's Samela!)

Pallas in wit,—all three, if you well view,
For beauty, wit, and matchless dignity
      Yield to Samela.

Robert Greene.

KINDS OF LOVE.

Foolish love is only folly;
Wanton love is too unholy;

Greedy love is covetous;
Idle love is frivolous;
But the gracious love is it
That doth prove the work of wit.

Beauty but deceives the eye;
Flattery leads the ear awry;
Wealth doth but enchant the wit;
Want, the overthrow of it;
While in Wisdom's worthy grace,
Virtue sees the sweetest face.

There hath Love found out his life,
Peace without all thought of strife;
Kindness in Discretion's care;
Truth, that clearly doth declare
Faith doth in true fancy prove,
Lust the excrements of Love.

Then in faith may fancy see
How my love may construed be;
How it grows and what it seeks;
How it lives and what it likes;
So in highest grace regard it,
Or in lowest scorn discard it.

Robert Greene.

LOVE AND BEAUTY.

Pretty twinkling starry eyes,
How did Nature first devise
Such a sparkling in your sight
As to give Love such delight,
As to make him like a fly,
Play with looks until he die?

Sure ye were not made at first
For such mischief to be curst;
As to kill Affection's care
That doth only truth declare;

Where worth's wonders never wither,
Love and Beauty live together.

Blessed eyes, then give your blessing,
That in passion's best expressing;
Love that only lives to grace ye,
May not suffer pride deface ye;
But in gentle thought's directions
Show the power of your perfections.

Robert Greene.

LOVE'S SERVILE LOT.

Love mistress is of many minds,
Yet few know whom they serve;
They reckon least how little hope
Their service doth deserve.

The will she robbeth from the wit,
The sense from reason's lore;
She is delightful in the rind,
Corrupted in the core.

May never was the month of love,
For May is full of flowers;
But rather April, wet by kind;
For love is full of showers.

With soothing words inthralled souls
She chains in servile bands!
Her eye in silence hath a speech
Which eye best understands.

Her little sweet hath many sours,
Short hap, immortal harms;
Her loving looks are murdering darts,
Her songs bewitching charms.

Like winter rose, and summer ice,
Her joys are still untimely;
Before her hope, behind remorse,
Fair first, in fine unseemly.

Plough not the seas, sow not the sands,
Leave off your idle pain;
Seek other mistress for your minds,
Love's service is in vain.

Robert Southwell.

THE HEART OF STONE.

Whence comes my love? O heart, disclose!
It was from cheeks that shame the rose,
From lips that spoil the ruby's praise,
From eyes that mock the diamond's blaze:
Whence comes my woe? as freely own;
Ah me! 'twas from a heart like stone.

The blushing cheek speaks modest mind,
The lips befitting words most kind,
The eye does tempt to love's desire,
And seems to say, "'Tis Cupid's fire;"
Yet all so fair but speak my moan,
Since nought doth say the heart of stone.

Why thus, my love, so kind bespeak
Sweet eye, sweet lip, sweet blushing cheek, —
Yet not a heart to save my pain?
O Venus, take thy gifts again!
Make not so fair to cause our moan,
Or make a heart that's like your own.

John Harrington.

A SHEPHERD'S SONG TO HIS LOVE.

Diaphenia, like the daffa-down-dilly,
White as the sun, fair as the lily,
  Heigh-ho, how I do love thee!
I do love thee as my lambs
Are beloved of their dams:
  How blest I were if thou would'st prove me!

Diaphenia, like the spreading roses,
That in thy sweets all sweets encloses,
  Fair sweet, how I do love thee!
I do love thee as each flower
Loves the sun's life-giving power;
  For, dead, thy breath to life might move me.

Diaphenia, like to all things blessed,
When all thy praises are expressed,
  Dear joy, how I do love thee!
As the birds do love the spring,
Or the bees their careful king:
  Then, in requite, sweet virgin, love me!

Henry Constable.

LOVE NOW, FOR ROSES FADE.

Look, Delia, how we esteem the half-blown rose,
The image of thy blush, and summer's honour!
Whilst yet her tender bud doth undisclose
That full of beauty Time bestows upon her:
No sooner spreads her glory in the air,
But straight her wide-blown pomp comes to decline;
She then is scorn'd, that late adorn'd the fair.
So fade the roses of those cheeks of thine!

No April can revive thy withered flowers,
Whose springing grace adorns thy glory now:
Swift speedy Time, feathered with flying hours,
Dissolves the beauty of the fairest brow.
  Then do not thou such treasure waste in vain,
  But love now, whilst thou may'st be loved again.

Samuel Daniel.

EARLY LOVE.

Ah! I remember well (and how can I
But evermore remember well) when first
Our flame began, when scarce we knew what was
The flame we felt; when as we sat and sigh'd
And look'd upon each other, and conceived
Not what we ail'd—yet something we did ail;
And yet were well, and yet we were not well,
And what was our disease we could not tell.
Then would we kiss, then sigh, then look; and thus
In that first garden of our simpleness
We spent our childhood. But when years began
To reap the fruit of knowledge, ah, how then
Would she with graver looks, with sweet, stern brow,
Check my presumption and my forwardness;
  Yet still would give me flowers, still would me show
  What she would have me, yet not have me know.

Samuel Daniel.

LOVE IS A SICKNESS.

Love is a sickness full of woes,
  All remedies refusing;
A plant that most with cutting grows,
  Most barren with best using.
        Why so?
More we enjoy it, more it dies,
  If not enjoyed, it sighing cries,
        Heigh-ho!

Love is a torment of the mind,
  A tempest everlasting;
And Jove hath made it of a kind
  Not well, nor full nor fasting.
        Why so?
More we enjoy it, more it dies,
  If not enjoyed, it sighing cries,
        Heigh-ho!

Samuel Daniel.

THE PASSIONATE SHEPHERD TO HIS LOVE.

Come live with me, and be my love,
And we will all the pleasures prove
That valleys, groves, and hills, and fields,
Woods or steepy mountain yields.

And we will sit upon the rocks,
Seeing the shepherds feed their flocks
By shallow rivers, to whose falls
Melodious birds sing madrigals.

And I will make thee beds of roses,
And a thousand fragrant posies:
A cap of flowers, and a kirtle,
Embroider'd all with leaves of myrtle.

A gown made of the finest wool,
Which from our pretty lambs we'll pull;
Fair lined slippers for the cold,
With buckles of the purest gold.

A belt of straw and ivy buds,
With coral clasps and amber studs:
And if these pleasures may thee move,
Come live with me and be my love.

The shepherd swains shall dance and sing
For thy delight each May morning.
If these delights thy mind may move,
Come live with me and be my love.

Christopher Marlowe.

[See "The Shepherdess's Reply to The Passionate Pilgrim,".]

LOVE'S OMNIPRESENCE.

Were I as base as is the lowly plain,
And you, my Love, as high as heaven above,
Yet should the thoughts of me your humble swain
Ascend to heaven, in honour of my Love.

Were I as high as heaven above the plain,
And you, my Love, as humble and as low
As are the deepest bottoms of the main,
Whereso'er you were, with you my love should go.

Were you the earth, dear Love, and I the skies,
My love should shine on you like to the sun,
And look upon you with ten thousand eyes
Till heaven wax'd blind, and till the world were done.

Whereso'er I am, below, or else above you,
Whereso'er you are, my heart shall truly love you.

J. Sylvester.

A PARTING; OR, LOVE'S LAST CHANCE.

Since there's no help, come let us kiss and part:
  Nay, I have done, you get no more of me;
And I am glad, yea, glad with all my heart,
  That thus so clearly I myself can free.
Shake hands for ever, cancel all our vows,
  And, when we meet at any time again,
Be it not seen in either of our brows
  That we one jot of former love retain.
Now, at the last gasp of Love's latest breath,
  When, his pulse failing, Passion speechless lies,
When Faith is kneeling by his bed of death,
  And Innocence is closing up his eyes;
Now, if thou wouldst, when all have given him over,
From death to life thou mightst him yet recover.

Michael Drayton.

WHO IS SILVIA?

Who is Silvia? What is she,
  That all our swains commend her?
Holy, fair, and wise is she:
  The heavens such grace did lend her,
That she might admired be.

Is she kind as she is fair?
  For beauty lives with kindness.
Love doth to her eyes repair
  To help him of his blindness,
And, being helped, inhabits there.

Then to Silvia let us sing,
  That Silvia is excelling;
She excels each mortal thing
  Upon the dull earth dwelling:
To her let us garlands bring.

William Shakespeare.

SIGH NO MORE, LADIES.

Sigh no more, ladies, sigh no more,
  Men were deceivers ever,
One foot in sea and one on shore,
  To one thing constant never:
    Then sigh not so,
    But let them go,
  And be you blithe and bonny,
Converting all your sounds of woe
  Into, Hey nonny, nonny.

Sing no more ditties, sing no moe
  Of dumps so dull and heavy;
The fraud of men was ever so,
  Since summer first was leafy.
    Then sigh not so,

But let them go,
And be you blithe and bonny,
Converting all your sounds of woe
Into, Hey nonny, nonny.

William Shakespeare.

A MORNING SONG FOR IMOGEN.

Hark! hark! the lark at heaven's gate sings,
And Phoebus 'gins arise';
His steeds to water at those springs
On chalic'd flowers that lies;
And winking Mary-buds begin
To ope their golden eyes:
With everything that pretty is,
My lady sweet arise:
Arise, arise.

William Shakespeare.

THE UNFAITHFUL SHEPHERDESS.

While that the sun with his beams hot
Scorched the fruits in vale and mountain,
Philon the shepherd, late forgot,
Sitting beside a crystal fountain,
  In shadow of a green oak tree
  Upon his pipe this song play'd he:
Adieu Love, adieu Love, untrue Love,
Untrue Love, untrue Love, adieu Love;
Your mind is light, soon lost for new love.

So long as I was in your sight
I was your heart, your soul, and treasure;
And evermore you sobb'd and sigh'd
Burning in flames beyond all measure:
  —Three days endured your love to me,
  And it was lost in other three!
Adieu Love, adieu Love, untrue Love,
Untrue Love, untrue Love, adieu Love;
Your mind is light, soon lost for new love.

Another Shepherd you did see
To whom your heart was soon enchained;
Full soon your love was leapt from me,
Full soon my place he had obtained.
  Soon came a third, your love to win,
  And we were out and he was in.
Adieu Love, adieu Love, untrue Love,
Untrue Love, untrue Love, adieu Love;
Your mind is light, soon lost for new love.

Sure you have made me passing glad
That you your mind so soon removed,
Before that I the leisure had
To choose you for my best beloved:
  For all your love was past and done
  Two days before it was begun:—
Adieu Love, adieu Love, untrue Love,
Untrue Love, untrue Love, adieu Love;
Your mind is light, soon lost for new love.

Anon., circa 1564.

TRUE LOVELINESS.

It is not Beauty I demand,
A crystal brow, the moon's despair,
Nor the snow's daughter, a white hand,
Nor mermaid's yellow pride of hair:

Tell me not of your starry eyes,
Your lips that seem on roses fed,
Your breasts, where Cupid tumbling lies,
Nor sleeps for kissing of his bed: —

A bloomy pair of vermeil cheeks,
Like Hebe's in her ruddiest hours,
A breath that softer music speaks
Than summer winds a-wooing flowers,

These are but gauds: nay, what are lips?
Coral beneath the ocean-stream,
Whose brink when your adventurer slips,
Full oft he perisheth on them.

And what are cheeks, but ensigns oft
That wave hot youth to fields of blood?
Did Helen's breast, though ne'er so soft,
Do Greece or Ilium any good?

Eyes can with baleful ardour burn;
Poison can breathe, that erst perfumed;
There's many a white hand holds an urn
With lovers' hearts to dust consumed.

For crystal brows there's nought within,
They are but empty cells for pride;
He who the Siren's hair would win
Is mostly strangled in the tide.

Give me, instead of Beauty's bust,
A tender heart, a loyal mind,
Which with temptation I would trust,
Yet never link'd with error find, —

One in whose gentle bosom I
Could pour my secret heart of woes,
Like the care-burthen'd honey-fly
That hides his murmurs in the rose, —

My earthly Comforter! whose love
So indefeasible might be,
That when my spirit wonn'd above,
Hers could not stay, for sympathy.

Anon.

A WOMAN'S REASON.

Love me not for comely grace,
For my pleasing eye or face,
Nor for any outward part;
No! nor for my constant heart, —
  For these may fail, or turn to ill;
  So thou and I shall sever:
Keep, therefore, a true woman's eye,
And love me well, but know not why.
  So hast thou the same reason still
  To dote upon me ever!

Anon.

LOVE WILL FIND OUT THE WAY.

Over the mountains
  And over the waves,
Under the fountains
  And under the graves;
Under floods that are deepest,
  Which Neptune obey;
Over rocks that are steepest,
  Love will find out the way.

Where there is no place

For the glow-worm to lie;
  Where there is no space
  For receipt of a fly;
Where the midge dares not venture,
  Lest herself fast she lay;
If love come, he will enter
  And soon find out his way.

You may esteem him
  A child for his might;
Or you may deem him
  A coward for his flight;
But if she whom Love doth honour
  Be concealed from the day,
Set a thousand guards upon her,
  Love will find out the way.

Some think to lose him
  By having him confin'd,
And some do suppose him,
  Poor thing, to be blind;
But if ne'er so close you wall him,
  Do the best that you may;
Blind Love, if so ye call him,
  Will find out his way.

You may train the eagle
  To stoop to your fist;
Or you may inveigle
  The Phoenix of the East;
The lioness, you may move her
  To give o'er her prey;
But you will never stop a lover —
  He will find out his way.

Anon.

PHILLIDA FLOUTS ME.

Oh, what a plague is love!
  I cannot bear it,

She will inconstant prove,
  I greatly fear it;
It so torments my mind,
  That my heart faileth,
She wavers with the wind,
  As a ship saileth;
Please her the best I may,
  She looks another way;
Alack and well a-day!
  Phillida flouts me.

I often heard her say
  That she loved posies:
In the last month of May
  I gave her roses,
Cowslips and gillyflow'rs
  And the sweet lily,
I got to deck the bow'rs
  Of my dear Philly;
She did them all disdain,
  And threw them back again;
Therefore, 'tis flat and plain
  Phillida flouts me.

Which way soe'er I go,
  She still torments me;
And whatsoe'er I do,
  Nothing contents me:
I fade, and pine away
  With grief and sorrow;
I fall quite to decay,
  Like any shadow;
Since 'twill no better be,
  I'll bear it patiently;
Yet all the world may see
  Phillida flouts me.

Circa 1610.

IN PRAISE OF TWO.

Faustina hath the fairest face,
And Phillida the better grace;
  Both have mine eye enriched:
This sings full sweetly with her voice;
Her fingers make so sweet a noise:
  Both have mine ear bewitched.
Ah me! sith Fates have so provided,
My heart, alas! must be divided.

Anon.

TO HIS FORSAKEN MISTRESS.

I do confess thou'rt smooth and fair,
  And I might have gone near to love thee,
Had I not found the slightest prayer
  That lips could speak, had power to move thee;
But I can let thee now alone,
As worthy to be loved by none.

I do confess thou'rt sweet, but find
  Thee such an unthrift of thy sweets,
Thy favours are but like the wind,
  That kisses everything it meets;
And since thou can with more than one,
Thou'rt worthy to be kiss'd by none.

The morning rose that untouch'd stands,
  Arm'd with her briars, how sweetly smells;
But, pluck'd and strain'd through ruder hands,
  Her sweet no longer with her dwells.
But scent and beauty both are gone,
And leaves fall from her, one by one.

Such fate ere long will thee betide,
  When thou hast handled been a while;
Like sere flowers to be thrown aside;—
  And I will sigh, while some will smile,
To see thy love for more than one
Hath brought thee to be loved by none.

Sir Robert Aytoun.

ON WOMAN'S INCONSTANCY.

I Lov'd thee once, I'll love no more,
  Thine be the grief as is the blame;
Thou art not what thou wert before,
  What reason I should be the same?
  He that can love unlov'd again,

Hath better store of love than brain:
God send me love my debts to pay,
While unthrifts fool their love away.

Nothing could have my love o'erthrown,
  If thou hadst still continued mine;
Yea, if thou hadst remain'd thy own,
  I might perchance have yet been thine.
    But thou thy freedom did recall,
    That if thou might elsewhere inthral;
  And then how could I but disdain
  A captive's captive to remain?

When new desires had conquer'd thee,
  And chang'd the object of thy will,
It had been lethargy in me,
  Not constancy to love thee still.
    Yea it had been a sin to go
    And prostitute affection so,
  Since we are taught no prayers to say
  To such as must to others pray.

Yet do thou glory in thy choice,
  Thy choice of his good fortune's boast;
I'll neither grieve nor yet rejoice
  To see him gain what I have lost;
    The height of my disdain shall be,
    To laugh at him, to blush for thee;
  To love thee still, but go no more
  A-begging to a beggar's door.

Sir Robert Aytoun.

THE THREE STATES OF WOMAN.

In a maiden-time profess'd,
Then we say that life is bless'd;
Tasting once the married life,
Then we only praise the wife;
There's but one state more to try,
Which makes women laugh or cry —
Widow, widow: of these three
The middle's best, and that give me.

Thomas Middleton.

MY LOVE AND I MUST PART.

Weep eyes, break heart!
My love and I must part.
Cruel fates true love do soonest sever;
O, I shall see thee never, never, never!
O, happy is the maid whose life takes end
Ere it knows parent's frown or loss of friend!
Weep eyes, break heart!
My love and I must part.

Thomas Middleton.

PERFECT BEAUTY.

It was a beauty that I saw,
  So pure, so perfect, as the frame
  Of all the universe was lame,
To that one figure, could I draw,
Or give least line of it a law!
  A skein of silk without a knot,
A fair march made without a halt,
A curious form without a fault,
  A printed book without a blot,
  All beauty, and without a spot!

Ben Jonson.

TO CELIA.

Drink to me only with thine eyes,
  And I will pledge with mine;
Or leave a kiss but in the cup,
  And I'll not look for wine.
The thirst that from the soul doth rise
  Doth ask a drink divine;
But might I of Jove's nectar sup,
  I would not change for thine.

I sent thee late a rosy wreath,
  Not so much honouring thee
As giving it a hope that there
  It could not withered be:
But thou thereon didst only breathe
  And sent'st it back to me;
Since when it grows, and smells, I swear,
  Not of itself, but thee!

Ben Jonson.

A WOMAN'S CONSTANCY.

Now thou hast loved me one whole day,
To-morrow, when thou leav'st, what wilt thou say?
Wilt thou then ante-date some new-made vow?
　Or say, that now
We are not just those persons which we were?
Or, that oaths made in reverential fear
Of Love and his wrath any may forswear?
　Or, as true deaths true marriages untie,
So lovers' contracts, images of those,
Bind but till Sleep, Death's image, them unloose?
　Or, your own end to justify
For having purposed change and falsehood, you
Can have no way but falsehood to be true?
Vain lunatic! Against these scapes I could
　Dispute and conquer if I would;
Which I abstain to do;
For, by to-morrow, I may think so too.

Dr. John Donne.

SWEETEST LOVE.

Sweetest love, I do not go
For weariness of thee,
Nor in hope the world can show
A fitter love for me.
But since that I
Must die at last, 'tis best
Thus to use myself in jest
By feigned death to die.

Yester-night the sun went hence,
And yet is here to-day;
He hath no desire nor sense,
Nor half so short a way:
Then fear not me,
But believe that I shall make

Hastier journeys, since I take
More wings and spurs than he.

Dr. John Donne.

TO AURORA.

O if thou knew'st how thou thyself dost harm,
And dost prejudge thy bliss, and spoil my rest;
Then would'st thou melt the ice out of thy breast,
And thy relenting heart would kindly warm.
O, if thy pride did not our joys control,
What world of loving wonders should'st thou see!
For if I saw thee once transform'd in me,
Then in thy bosom I would pour my soul;
Then all my thoughts should in thy visage shine,
And if that aught mischanced thou should'st not moan
Nor bear the burthen of thy griefs alone:
No, I would have my share in what were thine:
  And whilst we thus should make our sorrows one,
  This happy harmony would make them none.

W. Alexander, Earl of Stirling.

PHILLIS.

In petticoat of green,
Her hair about her eyne,
Phillis, beneath an oak,
Sat milking her fair flock.
'Mongst that sweet-strained moisture, rare delight!
Her hand seem'd milk, in milk it was so white.

William Drummond.

TAKE THOSE LIPS AWAY.

Take, O, take those lips away,
  That so sweetly were forsworn;
And those eyes, the break of day,
  Lights that do mislead the morn:
But my kisses bring again, bring again;
Seals of love, but sealed in vain, sealed in vain.

Hide, O, hide those hills of snow,
  Which thy frozen bosom bears,
On whose tops the pinks that grow
  Are of those that April wears;
But first set my poor heart free,
Bound in icy chains by thee.

Beaumont and Fletcher.

TELL ME, WHAT IS LOVE?

Tell me, dearest, what is love?
'Tis a lightning from above,
'Tis an arrow, 'tis a fire,
'Tis a boy they call Desire.
    'Tis a grave
    Gapes to have
Those poor fools that long to prove.

Tell me more, are women true?
Yes, some are, and some as you;
Some are willing, some are strange,
Since you men first taught to change.
    And till truth
    Be in both
All shall love to love anew.

Tell me more yet, can they grieve?
Yes, and sicken sore, but live:
And be wise and delay,
When you men are as wise as they.
    Then I see
    Faith will be
Never till they both believe.

Francis Beaumont.

PINING FOR LOVE.

How long shall I pine for love?
  How long shall I sue in vain?
How long like the turtle-dove,
  Shall I heartily thus complain?
Shall the sails of my heart stand still?
  Shall the grists of my hope be unground?
Oh fie, oh fie, oh fie,
  Let the mill, let the mill go round.

Francis Beaumont.

FIE ON LOVE.

Now fie on foolish love, it not befits
  Or man or woman know it.
Love was not meant for people in their wits,
  And they that fondly show it
Betray the straw, and features in their brain,
And shall have Bedlam for their pain:
If simple love be such a curse,
To marry is to make it ten times worse.

Francis Beaumont.

DAMOETAS' PRAISE OF HIS DAPHNIS.

Tune on my pipe the praises of my love,
   Love fair and bright;
Fill earth with sound, and airy heavens above,
   Heavens Jove's delight,
    With Daphnis' praise.

Her tresses are like wires of beaten gold,
   Gold bright and sheen;
Like Nisus' golden hair that Scylla poll'd,
   Scyll o'erseen
    Through Minos' love.

Her eyes like shining lamps in midst of night,
   Night dark and dead:
Or as the stars that give the seamen light,
   Light for to lead
    Their wandering ships.

Amidst her cheeks the rose and lily strive,
   Lily snow-white:
When their contest doth make their colour thrive,
   Colour too bright
    For shepherds' eyes.

Her lips like scarlet of the finest dye,
   Scarlet blood-red:
Teeth white as snow, which on the hills do lie,
   Hills overspread
    By winter's force.

Her skin as soft as is the finest silk,
   Silk soft and fine:
Of colour like unto the whitest milk,
   Milk of the kine
    Of Daphnis' herd.

As swift of foot as is the pretty roe,
   Roe swift of pace:
When yelping hounds pursue her to and fro,

Hounds fierce in chase
To reave her life.

Cease to tell of any more compare,
    Compares too rude,
Daphnis' deserts and beauty are too rare:
    Then here conclude
    Fair Daphnis' praise.

John Wootton.

SHALL I, WASTING IN DESPAIR?

Shall I, wasting in despair,
Die because a woman's fair?
Or my cheeks make pale with care,
'Cause another's rosy are?
Be she fairer than the day,
Or the flowery meads in May,
  If she be not so to me,
  What care I how fair she be?

Shall my foolish heart be pined
'Cause I see a woman kind;
Or a well-disposed nature
Joined with a lovely feature?
Be she meeker, kinder, than
Turtle-dove or pelican,
  If she be not so to me,
  What care I how kind she be?

Shall a woman's virtues move
Me to perish for her love?
Or her merit's value known,
Make me quite forget mine own?
Be she with that goodness blest
Which may gain her name of Best;
  If she seem not such to me,
  What care I how good she be?

'Cause her fortune seems too high,
Shall I play the fool and die?
Those that bear a noble mind,
Where they want, of riches find.
Think what with them they would do
Who without them dare to woo:
  And unless that mind I see,
  What care I tho' great she be?

Great or good, or kind or fair,
I will ne'er the more despair;
If she love me, this believe,

I will die ere she shall grieve;
If she slight me when I woo,
I can scorn and let her go;
  For if she be not for me,
  What care I for whom she be?

George Wither.

TO ONE WHO, WHEN I PRAISED MY MISTRESS'S BEAUTY, SAID I WAS BLIND.

Wonder not, though I am blind,
    For you must be
Dark in your eyes, or in your mind,
    If, when you see
Her face, you prove not blind like me;
If the powerful beams that fly
    From her eye,
And those amorous sweets that lie
Scatter'd in each neighbouring part,
Find a passage to your heart,
Then you'll confess your mortal sight
Too weak for such a glorious light:
For if her graces you discover,
You grow, like me, a dazzled lover;
But if those beauties you not spy,
Then are you blinder far than I.

Thomas Carew.

HE THAT LOVES A ROSY CHEEK

He that loves a rosy cheek,
  Or a coral lip admires,
Or from star-like eyes doth seek
  Fuel to maintain his fires;
As old Time makes these decay,
So his flames must waste away.

But a smooth and steadfast mind,
  Gentle thoughts and calm desires,
Hearts with equal love combined,
  Kindle never-dying fires;
Where these are not, I despise
Lovely cheeks, or lips, or eyes.

Thomas Carew.

MATIN SONG.

Rise, Lady Mistress! rise!
  The night hath tedious been;
No sleep hath fallen into mine eyes,
  Nor slumbers made me sin.
Is not she a saint, then, say!
Thought of whom keeps sin away?

Rise, madam! rise, and give me light,
  Whom darkness still will cover,
And ignorance, more dark than night,
  Till thou smile on thy lover.
All want day till thy beauty rise,
For the gray morn breaks from thine eyes.

Nathaniel Field.

JULIA.

Some asked me where the rubies grew,
  And nothing did I say,
But with my finger pointed to
  The lips of Julia.

Some asked how pearls did grow, and where;
  Then spake I to my girl,
To part her lips and show me there
  The quarelets of pearl.

One asked me where the roses grew;
  I bade him not go seek,
But forthwith bade my Julia show
  A bud in either cheek.

Robert Herrick.

CHERRY RIPE.

"Cherry ripe, ripe, ripe," I cry,
"Full and fair ones—come and buy;"
If so be you ask me where
They do grow? I answer, "There,
Where my Julia's lips do smile;"
There's the land, or cherry-isle,
Whose plantations fully show
All the year where cherries grow!

Robert Herrick.

TO THE VIRGINS.

Gather ye rosebuds while ye may,
  Old Time is still a-flying;
And this same flower that smiles to-day,

To-morrow will be dying.

The glorious lamp of heaven, the sun,
  The higher he's a-getting,
The sooner will his race be run,
  And nearer he's to setting.

That age is best which is the first,
  When youth and blood are warmer;
But being spent, the worse and worst
  Times still succeed the former.

Then be not coy, but use your time,
  And while ye may, go marry;
For having lost but once your prime,
  You may for ever tarry.

Robert Herrick.

TO ELECTRA.

I dare not ask a kiss;
  I dare not beg a smile;
Lest having that or this,
  I might grow proud the while.

No, no, the utmost share
  Of my desire shall be,
Only to kiss that air
  That lately kissed thee.

Robert Herrick.

DRY THOSE EYES.

Dry those fair, those crystal eyes,
Which like growing fountains rise
To drown their banks! Grief's sullen brooks
Would better flow in furrow'd looks:
Thy lovely face was never meant
To be the shore of discontent.

Then clear those waterish stars again,
Which else portend a lasting rain;
Lest the clouds which settle there
Prolong my winter all the year,
And thy example others make
In love with sorrow, for thy sake.

Dr. Henry King.

LOVE'S CONSTANCY.

Dear, if you change, I'll never choose again;
Sweet, if you shrink, I'll never think of love;
Fair, if you fail, I'll judge all beauty vain;
Wise, if too weak, more wits I'll never prove.
Dear, sweet, fair, wise,—change, shrink, nor be not weak;
And, on my faith, my faith shall never break.

Earth with her flowers shall sooner heaven adorn;
Heaven her bright stars through earth's dim globe shall move;
Fire heat shall lose, and frosts of flames be born;
Air, made to shine, as black as hell shall prove:
Earth, heaven, fire, air, the world transformed shall view,
Ere I prove false to faith, or strange to you.

John Dowland.

FAREWELL, MY JOY.

Farewell! my joy!
  Adieu! my love and pleasure!
To sport and toy
  We have no longer leisure.
      Fa la la!

Farewell! adieu!
  Until our next consorting!
Sweet love, be true!
  And thus we end our sporting.
      Fa la la!

Thomas Weelkes.

THE LARK NOW LEAVES HIS WAT'RY NEST.

The lark now leaves his wat'ry nest,
  And climbing, shakes his dewy wings,
He takes your window for the east,
  And to implore your light, he sings;
Awake, awake, the morn will never rise
Till she can dress her beauty at your eyes.

The merchant bows unto the seaman's star,
  The ploughman from the sun his season takes;
But still the lover wonders what they are,
  Who look for day before his mistress wakes.
Awake, awake, break through your veils of lawn,
Then draw your curtains, and begin the dawn.

Sir William Davenant.

GO, LOVELY ROSE.

Go, lovely Rose,
Tell her that wastes her time and me,
That now she knows
When I resemble her to thee,
How sweet and fair she seems to be.

Tell her that's young,
And shuns to have her graces spied,
That had'st thou sprung
In deserts where no men abide,
Thou must have uncommended died.

Small is the worth
Of beauty from the light retired;
Bid her come forth,
Suffer herself to be desired,
And not blush so to be admired.

Then die, that she
The common fate of all things rare
May read in thee,
How small a part of time they share
Who are so wondrous sweet and fair!

Edmund Waller.

HIS MISTRESS.

I have a mistress, for perfections rare
In every eye, but in my thoughts most fair.
Like tapers on the altar shine her eyes;
Her breath is the perfume of sacrifice.
And wheresoe'er my fancy would begin,
Still her perfection lets religion in.
We sit and talk, and kiss away the hours
As chastely as the morning dews kiss flowers.
I touch her, like my beads, with devout care,
And come unto my courtship as my prayer.

Thomas Randolph.

CHLORIS.

Amyntas, go! Thou art undone,
  Thy faithful heart is crossed by fate;
That love is better not begun,
  Where love is come to love too late.

Yet who that saw fair Chloris weep
  Such sacred dew, with such pure grace,
Durst think them feigned tears, or seek
  For treason in an angel's face.

Henry Vaughan.

LOVE ME LITTLE, LOVE ME LONG.

Love me little, love me long,
  Is the burden of my song;
Love that is too hot and strong
  Burneth soon to waste;
Still I would not have thee cold,
  Or backward, or too bold,
For love that lasteth till 'tis old
  Fadeth not in haste.

Winter's cold, or summer's heat,
  Autumn tempests on it beat,
It can never know defeat,
  Never can rebel;
Such the love that I would gain,
  Such love, I tell thee plain,
That thou must give or love in vain,
  So to thee farewell.

Circa 1610.

FAIN WOULD I CHANGE THAT NOTE.

Fain would I change that note
To which fond love hath charm'd me,
Long, long to sing by rote,
Fancying that that harm'd me:
Yet when this thought doth come,
"Love is the perfect sum
Of all delight,"
I have no other choice
Either for pen or voice
To sing or write.

O Love, they wrong thee much
That say thy sweet is bitter,
When thy rich fruit is such
As nothing can be sweeter.
Fair house of joy and bliss
Where truest pleasure is,
I do adore thee;
I know thee what thou art,
I serve thee with my heart,
And fall before thee.

Captain Tobias Hume.

TO ROSES IN CASTARA'S BREAST.

Ye blushing Virgins happy are
  In the chaste Nunn'ry of her breasts,
For he'd profane so chaste a fair,
  Whoe'er should call them Cupid's nests.

Transplanted thus how bright ye grow,
  How rich a perfume do ye yield?
In some close garden, cowslips so
  Are sweeter than in th' open field.

In those white Cloisters live secure
  From the rude blasts of wanton breath,
Each hour more innocent and pure,
  Till you shall wither into death.

Then that which living gave you room,
  Your glorious sepulchre shall be;
There wants no marble for a tomb,
  Whose breast hath marble been to me.

William Habington.

THOU PRETTY BIRD.

Thou pretty bird, how do I see
Thy silly state and mine agree!
For thou a prisoner art;
  So is my heart.
Thou sing'st to her, and so do I address
My music to her ear that's merciless;
But herein doth the difference lie, —
That thou art graced; so am not I;
Thou singing livest, and I must singing die.

John Danyel.

ONCE I LOV'D A MAIDEN FAIR.

Once I lov'd a maiden fair,
  But she did deceive me;
She with Venus might compare,
  In my mind, believe me:
She was young, and among
  All our maids the sweetest.
Now I say, ah! well-a-day!
  Brightest hopes are fleetest.

I the wedding ring had got,
  Wedding clothes provided,
Sure the church would bind a knot
  Ne'er to be divided:
Married we straight must be,
  She her vows had plighted;
Vows, alas! as frail as glass:
  All my hopes are blighted.

Maidens wav'ring and untrue,
  Many a heart have broken;
Sweetest lips the world e'er knew,
  Falsest words have spoken.
Fare thee well, faithless girl,
  I'll not sorrow for thee;
Once I held thee dear as pearl,
  Now I do abhor thee.

Temp. Jas. I. (condensed by T. Oxenford).

I PR'YTHEE SEND ME BACK MY HEART.

I pr'ythee send me back my heart,
  Since I cannot have thine;
For if from yours you will not part,
  Why then shouldst thou have mine?

Yet now I think on't, let it lie;
  To find it were in vain,
For thou'st a thief in either eye
  Would steal it back again.

Why should two hearts in one breast lie,
  And yet not lodge together?
O love! where is thy sympathy,
  If thus our breasts you sever?

But love is such a mystery,
  I cannot find it out;
For when I think I'm best resolved,
  I then am most in doubt.

Then farewell love, and farewell woe,
  I will no longer pine;
For I'll believe I have her heart
  As much as she hath mine.

Sir John Suckling.

ORSAMES' SONG.

Why so pale and wan, fond lover?
  Prithee, why so pale?
Will, when looking well can't move her,
  Looking ill prevail?
  Prithee, why so pale?

Why so dull and mute, young sinner?
  Prithee, why so mute?

Will, when speaking well can't win her,
    Saying nothing do't?
    Prithee, why so mute?

Quit, quit, for shame, this will not move,
    This cannot take her;
If of herself she will not love,
    Nothing can make her:
    The devil take her!

Sir John Suckling.

SINCE FIRST I SAW YOUR FACE.

Since first I saw your face I resolved
  To honour and renown you;
If now I be disdained
  I wish my heart had never known you.
What! I that loved, and you that liked,
  Shall we begin to wrangle?
No, no, no, my heart is fast
  And cannot disentangle.

The sun whose beams most glorious are,
  Rejecteth no beholder,
And your sweet beauty past compare,
  Made my poor eyes the bolder.
Where beauty moves, and wit delights
  And signs of kindness bind me,
There, oh! there, where'er I go
  I leave my heart behind me.

If I admire or praise you too much,
  That fault you may forgive me,
Or if my hands had strayed but a touch,
  Then justly might you leave me.
I asked you leave, you bade me love;
  Is't now a time to chide me?
No, no, no, I'll love you still,
  What fortune e'er betide me.

Circa 1617.

THE GIVEN HEART.

I Wonder what those lovers mean, who say
They've given their hearts away.
Some good, kind lover, tell me how:
For mine is but a torment to me now.

If so it be one place both hearts contain,
For what do they complain?
What courtesy can Love do more,
Than to join hearts that parted were before?

Woe to her stubborn heart, if once mine come
Into the self-same room;
'Twill tear and blow up all within
Like a grenade shot into a magazine.

Then shall Love keep the ashes and torn parts
Of both our broken hearts;
Shall out of both one new one make,
From hers th' alloy, from mine the metal take.

For of her heart he from the flames will find
But little left behind:
Mine only will remain entire,
No dross was there to perish in the fire.

Abraham Cowley.

ICE AND FIRE.

Naked Love did to thine eye,
Chloris, once to warm him, fly;
But its subtle flame, and light,
Scorch'd his wings, and spoiled his sight.

Forc'd from thence he went to rest
In the soft couch of thy breast:
But there met a frost so great,
As his torch extinguish'd straight.

When poor Cupid (thus constrain'd
His cold bed to leave) complain'd:
"'Las! what lodging's here for me,
If all ice and fire she be."

Sir Edmund Sherburne.

AMARANTHA.

Amarantha, sweet and fair,
Forbear to braid that shining hair;
As my curious hand or eye,
Hovering round thee, let it fly:

Let it fly as unconfined
As its ravisher the wind,
Who has left his darling east
To wanton o'er this spicy nest.

Every tress must be confess'd
But neatly tangled at the best,
Like a clew of golden thread,
Most excellently ravelled.

Do not then wind up that light
In ribands, and o'ercloud the night;
Like the sun in his early ray,
But shake your head and scatter day.

Richard Lovelace.

TO ALTHEA, FROM PRISON.

When love, with unconfined wings,
  Hovers within my gates,
And my divine Althea brings
  To whisper at the grates;
When I lie tangled in her hair,
  And fetter'd to her eye—
The birds that wanton in the air,
  Know no such liberty.

  *   *   *   *   *

Stone walls do not a prison make,
  Nor iron bars a cage;

Minds innocent and quiet take
  That for an hermitage.
If I have freedom in my love,
  And in my soul am free, —
Angels alone, that soar above,
  Enjoy such liberty.

Richard Lovelace.

A MOCK SONG.

Tis true I never was in love:
  But now I mean to be,
    For there's no art
    Can shield a heart
  From love's supremacy.

Though in my nonage I have seen
  A world of taking faces,
I had not age or wit to ken
  Their several hidden graces.

Those virtues which, though thinly set,
  In others are admired,
In thee are altogether met,
  Which make thee so desired.

That though I never was in love,
  Nor never meant to be,
    Thyself and parts
    Above my arts
  Have drawn my heart to thee.

Alexander Brome.

SPEAKING AND KISSING.

The air which thy smooth voice doth break,
  Into my soul like lightning flies;
My life retires while thou dost speak,
  And thy soft breath its room supplies.

Lost in this pleasing ecstasy,
  I join my trembling lips to thine,
And back receive that life from thee
  Which I so gladly did resign.

Forbear, Platonic fools! t' inquire
  What numbers do the soul compose;
No harmony can life inspire
  But that which from these accents flows.

Thomas Stanley.

LADIES' CONQUERING EYES.

Ladies, though to your conquering eyes
Love owes its chiefest victories,
And borrows those bright arms from you
With which he does the world subdue;
Yet you yourselves are not above
The empire nor the griefs of love.

Then rack not lovers with disdain,
Lest love on you revenge their pain:
You are not free because you're fair,
The Boy did not his mother spare:
Though beauty be a killing dart,
It is no armour for the heart.

George Etherege.

DORINDA.

Dorinda's sparkling wit and eyes,
  United, cast too fierce a light,
Which blazes high, but quickly dies,
  Pains not the heart, but hurts the sight.

Love is a calmer, gentler joy,
  Smooth are his looks and soft his pace;
Her Cupid is a blackguard boy
  That runs his link full in your face.

Charles Sackville.

CELIA AND SYLVIA.

Celia is cruel. Sylvia, thou,
  I must confess art kind;
But in her cruelty, I vow,
  I more repose can find.
For, oh! thy fancy at all games does fly,
Fond of address, and willing to comply.

Thus he that loves must be undone,
  Each way on rocks we fall;
Either you will be kind to none,
  Or worse, be kind to all.
Vain are our hopes, and endless is our care;
We must be jealous, or we must despair.

Robert Gould.

TRUE LOVE.

Love, when 'tis true, needs not the aid
　Of sighs, nor aches, to make it known,
And to convince the cruellest maid,
　Lovers should use their love alone.

Into their very looks 'twill steal,
　And he that most would hide his flame,
Does in that case his pain reveal:
　Silence itself can love proclaim.

Sir Charles Sedley.

TOO LATE!

Too late, alas! I must confess,
  You need not arts to move me;
Such charms by nature you possess,
  'Twere madness not to love ye.

Then spare a heart you may surprise,
  And give my tongue the glory
To boast, though my unfaithful eyes
  Betray a tender story.

John Wilmot, Earl of Rochester.

MY MISTRESS' HEART.

My dear mistress has a heart
  Soft as those kind looks she gave me;
When with Love's resistless art,
  And her eyes, she did enslave me.
But her constancy's so weak,
  She's so wild and apt to wander;
That my jealous heart would break
  Should we live one day asunder.

Melting joys about her move,
  Killing pleasures, wounding blisses;
She can dress her eyes in love,
  And her lips can arm with kisses.
Angels listen when she speaks,
  She's my delight, all mankind wonder;
But my jealous heart would break
  Should we live one day asunder.

John Wilmot, Earl of Rochester.

CONSTANCY.

I cannot change, as others do,
  Though you unjustly scorn;
Since the poor swain that sighs for you,
  For you alone was born.
No, Phillis, no, your heart to move
  A surer way I'll try;
And to revenge my slighted love,
  Will still love on and die.

When, killed with grief, Amyntas lies,
  And you to mind shall call
The sighs that now unpitied rise,
  The tears that vainly fall;
That welcome hour that ends his smart,
  Will then begin your pain;
For such a faithful tender heart
  Can never break in vain.

John Wilmot, Earl of Rochester.

MAN AND WOMAN.

Man is for woman made,
  And woman made for man;
As the spur is for the jade,
As the scabbard for the blade,
  As for liquor is the can,
So man's for woman made,
  And woman made for man.

As the sceptre to be sway'd,
As to night the serenade,
  As for pudding is the pan,
  As to cool us is the fan,
So man's for woman made,
  And woman made for man.

Peter Antony Motteux.

ACCEPT MY HEART.

Accept, my love, as true a heart
  As ever lover gave:
'Tis free, it vows, from any art,
  And proud to be your slave.

Then take it kindly, as 'twas meant,
  And let the giver live,
Who, with it, would the world have sent
  Had it been his to give.

And, that Dorinda may not fear
  I e'er will prove untrue,
My vow shall, ending with the year,
  With it begin anew.

Matthew Prior.

AN ANGELIC WOMAN.

Not an angel dwells above
Half so fair as her I love.
Heaven knows how she'll receive me:
If she smiles I'm blest indeed;
If she frowns I'm quickly freed;
Heaven knows she ne'er can grieve me.

None can love her more than I,
Yet she ne'er shall make me die,
If my flame can never warm her:
Lasting beauty I'll adore,
I shall never love her more,
Cruelty will so deform her.

Sir John Vanbrugh.

I SMILE AT LOVE.

I smile at Love, and all its arts,
  The charming Cynthia cried:
Take heed, for Love has piercing darts,
  A wounded swain replied.
Once free and blest as you are now,
  I trifled with his charms,
I pointed at his little bow,
  And sported with his arms,
Till urged too far, Revenge! he cries,
  A fatal shaft he drew,
It took its passage through your eyes,
  And to my heart it flew.

To tear it thence I tried in vain;
  To strive, I quickly found
Was only to increase the pain,
  And to enlarge the wound.
Ah! much too well, I fear, you know
  What pain I'm to endure,

Since what your eyes alone can do
  Your heart alone can cure.
And that (grant Heaven, I may mistake!)
  I doubt is doom'd to bear
A burden for another's sake,
  Who ill rewards its care.

Sir John Vanbrugh.

ADIEU L'AMOUR.

Here end my chains, and thraldom cease,
If not in joy, I'll live at least in peace;
Since for the pleasures of an hour,
We must endure an age of pain;
I'll be this abject thing no more,
Love, give me back my heart again.

Despair tormented first my breast,
Now falsehood, a more cruel guest;
O! for the peace of human kind,
Make women longer true, or sooner kind:
With justice, or with mercy reign,
O Love! or give me back my heart again.

George Granville.

SABINA WAKES.

See, see, she wakes! Sabina wakes!
  And now the sun begins to rise;
Less glorious is the morn that breaks
  From his bright beams, than her fair eyes.

With light united, day they give,
  But different fates ere night fulfil;
How many by his warmth will live!
  How many will her coldness kill!

William Congreve.

FALSE! OR INCONSTANCY.

False though she be to me and love,
  I'll ne'er pursue revenge;
For still the charmer I approve,
  Though I deplore her change.

In hours of bliss we oft have met,
  They could not always last;
And though the present I regret,
  I'm grateful for the past.

William Congreve.

LOVE AND HATE.

Why we love, and why we hate,
  Is not granted us to know:
Random chance, or wilful fate,
  Guides the shaft from Cupid's bow.

If on me Zelinda frown,
  Madness 'tis in me to grieve:
Since her will is not her own,
  Why should I uneasy live?

If I for Zelinda die,
  Deaf to poor Mizella's cries,
Ask not me the reason why:
  Seek the riddle in the skies.

Ambrose Philips.

I LATELY VOWED.

I lately vow'd, but 'twas in haste,
  That I no more would court
The joys that seem when they are past
  As dull as they are short.

I oft to hate my mistress swear,
  But soon my weakness find;
I make my oaths when she's severe,
  But break them when she's kind.

John Oldmixon.

FEW HAPPY MATCHES.

Say, mighty Love, and teach my song
To whom thy sweetest joys belong,
  And who the happy pairs
Whose yielding hearts, and joining hands,
Find blessings twisted with their bands
  To soften all their cares.

*   *   *   *   *

Two kindest souls alone must meet,
'Tis friendship makes the bondage sweet,
  And feeds their mutual loves:
Bright Venus on her rolling throne
Is drawn by gentlest birds alone,
  And Cupids yoke the doves.

Dr. Isaac Watts.

DORINDA'S CONQUEST.

Fame of Dorinda's conquest brought
  The God of Love her charms to view;
To wound th' unwary maid he thought,
  But soon became her conquest too.

He dropp'd half-drawn his feeble bow,
  He look'd, he raved, and sighing pined;
And wish'd in vain he had been now,
  As painters falsely draw him, blind.

Disarm'd, he to his mother flies;
  Help, Venus, help thy wretched son!
Who now will pay us sacrifice?
  For Love himself's, alas! undone.

To Cupid now no lover's prayer
  Shall be address'd in suppliant sighs;
My darts are gone, but, oh! beware,
  Fond mortals, of Dorinda's eyes!

John Hughes.

LOVERS IN DISGUISE.

How bless'd are lovers in disguise!
   Like gods, they see,
   As I do thee,
Unseen by human eyes.
   Exposed to view,
   I'm hid from view,
I'm altered, yet the same:
   The dark conceals me,
   Love reveals me:
Love, which lights me by its flame.

Were you not false, you would me know;
   For though your eyes
   Could not devise,
Your heart had told you so.
   Your heart would beat
   With eager heat,
And me by sympathy would find:
   True love might see,
   One changed like me,
False love is only blind.

George Farquhar.

WHEN THY BEAUTY APPEARS.

When thy beauty appears
In its graces and airs,
  All bright as an angel new dropt from the sky;
At a distance I gaze, and am aw'd by my fears,
  So strangely you dazzle my eye!

But then, without art,
Your kind thought you impart,
  When your love runs in blushes through every vein;
When it darts from your eyes, when it pants in your heart,
  Then I know you're a woman again.

There's a passion and pride
In our sex, she replied,
  And thus, might I gratify both, would I do:
Still an angel appear to each lover beside,
  But still be a woman to you.

Thomas Parnell.

Lightning Source UK Ltd.
Milton Keynes UK
UKHW010634140621
385483UK00001B/81